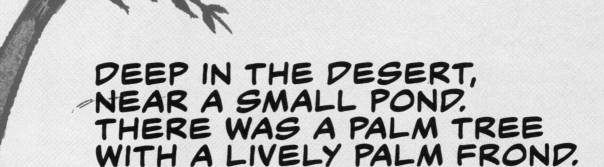

DEEP IN THE DESERT,
NEAR A SMALL POND.
THERE WAS A PALM TREE
WITH A LIVELY PALM FROND.

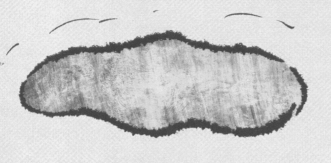

ONE LEAFLET WAS BIG,
AS WIDE AS CAN BE
"SAINT ANTONY WILL CLEARLY
SIT UNDER ME,

ANOTHER WAS LONGEST,
A WHOLE METER LONG!
"I'M OLDEST" IT SAID
"I'M MIGHTY AND STRONG.

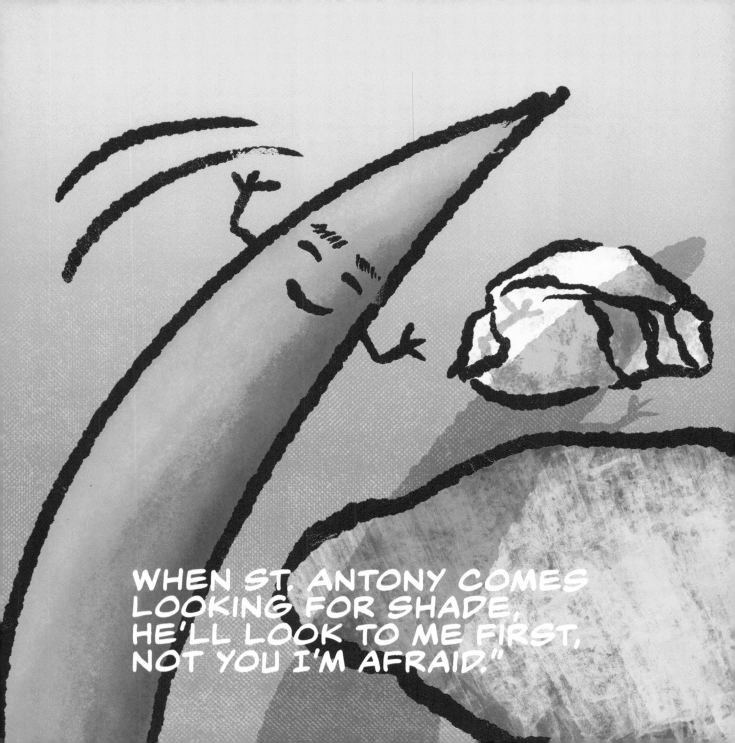

ONE LEAFLET WAS SAD,
ITS EYEBROWS DID SAG
"I'M YELLOW AND SMALL,
WITH NO REASON TO BRAG.

THE LEAFLETS ALL LAUGHED,
AND POINTED AT HIM.
THEY SAID "YOU'RE NOT STRONGER,
OR GREENER OR THIN."

THEY PUSHED AND THEY SHOVED
THE POOR LEAFLET AROUND
AND SINCE IT WAS WEAK,
IT SURELY FELL DOWN!

SAINT ANTONY WALKED UP,
AND STOPPED WHEN HE FOUND
THE WHITTLED LITTLE LEAFLET
THAT FELL TO THE GROUND.

HE PICKED UP THE LEAFLET,
WEAVED IT WITH CARE,
TO COMPLETE THE BASKET
HE TAKES EVERYWHERE.

THE LEAFLETS SAID "SORRY" TO THE ONE THEY DENIED AND LEARNED THEY SHOULD NOT GIVE IN TO THEIR PRIDE.

A PRAYER

DEAR SAINT ANTONY,

PRAY FOR US TO LOVE CHRIST LIKE YOU,
PUT HIM FIRST IN ALL THAT WE DO,
TEACH US HOW TO ALWAYS BE HUMBLE,
AND CLING TO GOD IF EVER WE FUMBLE!

AMEN.